Ghost Logic

FLOWSTONE PRESS
Illinois Valley, Oregon

Ghost Logic

Sara Clancy

Ghost Logic
Copyright © 2017 Sara Clancy
Winner, 2017 Turtle Island Editor's Choice Poetry Award

Turtle Island Quarterly sponsors the annual Turtle Island Poetry Awards. Awards are chosen by the editors. More information available at http://fourdirectionpoetry.wixsite.com/turtleisland

Cover photo "Rain on Glass 1" by William K. Kates
(Used with permission)

First Flowstone Press Edition, October 2017
ISBN-13 978-1-945824-14-2

for Rebecca

Table of Contents

Introduction, by Jared Smith	vii
Instead of a Common Brawl	3
The Zen of Jigsaw	4
Most Evenings She Searches for a Home	5
Viscera	6
What I Did for the Coyote Hunting My Dog	7
Prayer Wheel	8
The Pagoda on Yellowstone Highway	9
Tech Support from My House in Wyoming, 1999	10
The Poet Turns Las Vegas Into	11
Rattlesnake	12
My Father Refuses a Cane	13
Sand Painting	14
A Case for Ghosts	15
Cannibal	16
Family Geology	17
At Home with the Dead	18
Synesthete	19
Arrest Me Red	20
Against Economy	21
Mrs. Nation, Uninvited, Haunts "The Irma"	22
Right Behind You	23
Haboob	24
Wait Till the Scorpions Come Out	25
1962 Valiant Station Wagon	26
For Stella on the Day of the Dead	27
Stolen From My Father's Room	28
Sestina for Zayda and the Dogs	29
When the Test to Predict Alzheimer's Is Available	31

Introduction

by Jared Smith

Ghost Logic is somewhat like Quantum Physics in that once you have been introduced to it you learn how to think with an awareness that all things are knitted together eternally by smaller things that interact with each other across time and space, and you enter a world of immense complexity and beauty. Ghost Logic, however, is much more accessible because it explains itself in images and words rather than in numbers and equations. In short, this chapbook allows entry into a way of seeing and experiencing the world we are a part of in a way that few of us ever have a chance at, but once we have been touched by the mind that wrote these poems we will never be able to see the world the same way again.

This was not an easy book, intellectually or emotionally, for Sara Clancy to have written, rising not from celebration but from having to live through the physical and mental aging and passing of her father. Yet, the best advances in understanding come sadly enough from living through the greatest challenges that we face, and the greatest losses—those moments in time when we are forced to redefine the meaning of our lives to make life bearable. This is true in poetry as in any specialized form of human endeavor, and the path that Sara speaks of in Ghost Logic is one that we can all follow and grow from both before and after we ourselves encounter such challenges.

The structure of the individual poems is organic, short-lined imagist observational poems, and that structure is essential to the experience of the work as a whole. Each poem pulls apart, dissects, and gives enhanced meaning to the everyday objects and daily routines we surround ourselves with. Her visionary imagery expands those objects, giving them multiple meanings that become doorways into overlapping worlds and experiences we may not expect initially but which seem when discovered as inevitable. The solid crystal structure of the rocks we walk upon break apart in our hands—these wonders of nature with which we have built our industrial age—and are contrasted with the "ghosts of enterprise", the temporal and temporary items we slave over and the "tech support" where "I hear Manhattan in his voice" two thousand miles away while sitting at an open window before the open sky of Wyoming.

Sara's voice is not gentle. It rages against what cannot be changed:

> I put an iron bell in the wind
> over a pyramid of creosote, lit up
> with malice and hanging like God's own
> anvil in my naked allotment of sky

she writes in *What I Did for the Coyote Hunting My Dog*. But rather than letting the rage be its own end, she builds something hard and unwelcoming to that enemy that hunts what is hers. In that way she heals herself and those around her. And, from *Prayer Wheel*, "…maybe healing is an estuary," a birthplace and nursery into that vastness of the ocean that is beyond.

Of course, it is an estuary that many drown in. As she notes in *My Father Refuses a Cane*, "a fall can set the cogs of eternity/falling into each other one by one, while I try to fold his fingers/ around this rejected advocate/and call it some kind of faith."

There is a transcendence that comes through careful observation of all that is around us. It is possible to see clearly enough that one does not fall. There is a connection that can be made that keeps us and all we love alive. In *At Home with the Dead*, she writes, "yesterday is not gone and matters." And the sand that blows across our deserts and winnows its way through the crack beneath her door paints sacred images of our lives in eternity. Quoting from *Sand Painting*:

> I've locked the front door against dust,
> but it blows underneath and arranges itself
> into the prophecy of a Navajo painting,
> the beveled glass refracting caution
> on my newly stenciled slate.
>
> I will sweep this divination into the night,
> offer it like heated herbs to the bobcat who leaves
> me feathers in return. An appeasement to the pall
> of my mudroom…

What a poem, and what a book! Such a big world to hold between ones hands! But is there really a logic here? Yes, there is, for without a logic of sorts to hold these insights and feelings and observations together, there would be nothing really to learn from. But the logic is not the logic of our world of commerce. It is the logic of poetry… the spaces between images and stanzas that let you look at all things slowly and in a new light and juxtaposition. The ghost logic.

> To arrive here you need nothing
> like faith. Though I believe in memory
> don't you? These dubious apparitions
> insist on clarity…
>
> In the end I will trade the familiar
> cold spot with all its calibrations of doubt
> for evidence of your dazzling absence…
> your inexplicable breath
> warm and expired.
>
> from *A Case for Ghosts*

You will never leave this book behind. It will share new breath with you and will haunt you in very good ways.

Ghost Logic

Instead of a Common Brawl

Write a letter saying exactly
what you think, wrap it in silver
foil and throw it to the crow
strutting in your driveway.

Watch it ascend to a blue
so thin that your insults will
fire off one by one and float
down like lemon dust. Sweep
it into a black bowl and burn

it for its truth. Smudge your
fingers in the bile of this
incantation and write it out
again. This time under
the shelter of your skin

the tattoo of a just
and indifferent bird.

The Zen of Jigsaw

To put this devotional into context
find the edges and work against
confinement. To fill those spaces
with any preconceived afternoon

invites failure. Without the nuance
of focus on the yoga of minutiae
you may find yourself detached.
A warped cardboard tab separating

into a fan of frustration, you jam it home
between stone edges that won't line up,
a spark of red uncoupled from the sky
and missing the matrix of its dark wing.

Instead, imagine nothing
but what matches the rust around
the linchpin. The missing center
in the wheel of the Old Mill in Autumn.

Most Evenings She Searches for a Home

Tonight the fish-scale shingle Victorian
where icicles hang in horns of elemental fury
above grandmother's grey Valiant will prod
her to consider a Spanish prefab stucco tract
in the suburbs of Phoenix. She knows the grass
there is borrowed from the future and purple
clematis only flourish under the artificial drip
of the unsustainable optimism which she will trade

for a geodesic dome in Brattleboro, Vermont.
A pelican house is floating out of her reach
in the Chesapeake Bay, but there is also a fishing hut
on a lake in Germany, oblivious to its Brutalist
progeny. Both are supplanted by a school bus
in Denali she will share with the legend of a child
who starved common sense to nourish

a simple mistake. A blue walled house waits
for them both in the Namib Desert. It is filling up
with sand in deference to its twin yacht settling
underneath Antarctica. Perhaps a mill, a cooling tower
or a whole city would do. Like the rest it must
be vacated by stories and all the restless
tenants and ghosts of enterprise.

Viscera

There is such a thing as too
much beauty, you know.

By that I don't mean
the surrender of Scorpius
to the surface
of a summer pond,

or the crevasse,
loaned its blue
by an indifferent
wheeling sky.

I mean the vulnerability
of shale, broken open
to reveal its excruciating
history in quartz

or the moment
you offer up your
sad spent trust, like sweets
in an open bowl.

What I Did for the Coyote Hunting My Dog

I built him a lean-to
against the sun, made of caliche clay,
cactus ribs and remorse.

I walled in my kitchen garden
with wormwood, rue and coach whip skin
to keep out fellowship and the spiny
irony of omens that bloom at night.

I put an iron bell in the wind
over a pyramid of creosote, lit up
with malice and hanging like God's own
anvil in my naked allotment of sky.

Prayer Wheel

You have no illusions about the thing,
but the Sanskrit cast in copper and bronze
appeals like a pennyweight of promise,
a curiosity of metals, with your wish inside.

You can't pass without setting
it in motion. Nagging the fortunes
on his behalf, as if these exotic
accessories of belief can replace

the certainty of your indolent
reason, the weight of peer review
that concludes some double blind trial
with the hiss and ping of an ICU.

Which doesn't explain the dozens of times
you have read about doctors who said he would never
…and yet he did! The secular bulwarks simply fail
you here. Or maybe healing is an estuary

where logic meets optimism, if not faith,
if not the sheer, cussed determination
of hope cast to the gift on your coffee table,
spinning away from you, harming no one.

The Pagoda on Yellowstone Highway

If he could unbend the sky
then why not a system of pulleys
and ropes to catapult
his revelation
above Elephant Rock
like an ark?

We all agree
the structure is crazy
but the artist knows what we don't,
that gravity is a huckster,
that a misstep is currency
in the alchemy
of hammer and attitude
and that a man need be
left the hell alone.

Years later
when the wheelhouse
of his preposterous craft
is thick with soda cans and dust,
when tourists ask what on earth
it is and exactly
what he was thinking,

the injured air will right itself
and loan its baleful updraft
to the earthbound beams.

Tech Support from My House in Wyoming, 1999

There is always awkward small talk
on the restart. I can hear Manhattan
in his voice with its deadline urgency,
the beep and chimes of his computer as he fails
and reboots. Extensions load one by one
and we chat as we wait for my reconfiguration
to work or crash him out again.

He thinks my location is exotic
and he asks me what I see out my window.
I tell him there is a Common Night Hawk
circling in front of Jim Mountain and he whistles.
I ask the same. He snorts and tells me,
"Nothing like you see. I'm in the city.
Two pigeons. The North Tower."

The Poet Turns Las Vegas Into

a dandelion
dried by the desert to a sphere
any architect would admire.
It will pimp its reflection

to the duplicity of Lake Mead
before dispersing its payload
of want. Not a still-life

blossom, but a common weed,
precious as an inside straight,
the roots resolute

and propagated to every state,
the stems and leaves
supple with the color
of spectacle.

Rattlesnake

Despite a cautious advance
your startle reflex jumps
and stirs the nest hidden

between your revulsion and clumps
of barrel cactus by the patio.
That you dart away like a diamond

backed dilettante, whose longing
for a deciduous alternative,
you tell yourself, is instinct alone.

Or farce, when you mistake
the whip of an irrigation hose that lies
in calcified rust and pack rat shit,

a frown of contempt coiled
around your vase of lobelia
hissing its punch-line like a parody

of sin. Reminding you that hesitation
is an offense to the border between
what you thought was the refuge

of your fairy lit porch
and the twist of sinuous flight
that slips between your sandaled feet.

My Father Refuses a Cane

I tell myself recovery waits beside
the stick hanging on the bedside of his
new confinement and I tell him
that petulance is downright admirable.

The risk is believing angels
inhabit the framework of these small
improvements, a whispered
miracle we will never approach

seriously. These days his night light
is a holy thing when it reveals the hazard
of an unsteady path. He understands how
a fall can set the cogs of eternity

falling into each other one by one
while I try to fold his fingers
around this rejected advocate
and call it some kind of faith.

Sand Painting

I've locked the front door against dust,
but it blows underneath and arranges itself
into the prophesy of a Navajo painting,
the bezeled glass refracting caution
on my newly stenciled slate.

I will sweep this divination into the night,
offer it like heated herbs to the bobcat who leaves
me feathers in return. An appeasement to the pall
of my mudroom. I am sorry for that bird, her wasted
twigs a dry gift to my housekeeping. So I tell her

that the floor in my father's room
is so polished that he can't walk
without risk. He is offered slippers
to test his luck and a wheelchair
when it forfeits.

A Case for Ghosts

Though you think otherwise
I am aware of an intrusion into the day
that feels like any afternoon in reverse
where conversation is complete
recollection plays the radio
and we are all present.

To arrive here you need nothing
like faith. Though I believe in memory
don't you? These dubious apparitions
insist on clarity, if only the relief
of your forehead glimpsed against
the steady shade of my hand.

In the end I will trade the familiar
cold spot with all its calibrations of doubt
for evidence of your dazzling absence
in the instant you cool your coffee,
your inexplicable breath
warm and expired.

Cannibal

The bone that you used all winter
to pick the poison from your teeth
is mine and if you still crave that malice
you may find it in the iron caldron

of your appetite along with your own
empty ribs. You can season my bitter
epiphany by chanting our common
name to the host of this banquet

of forgery. Pray that your incantation
will not separate shared blood
from the meat of your famished intent.
In the name of your father. Amen.

Family Geology

The leaf behind the yellow aspen leaf is a lie.
The silver slingback in the corner of the closet
missing its tasteless mate is also a lie. Underneath
a heap of twigs is a new shrew's nest
built underneath the awning
of a lie.

The sonnet tucked into a book never read, the vial
of pills long expired, the measure of labor confirmed
by a time clock and photocopied with a signature line
for our approval all may be true,
but I doubt it.

The whole account is suspect, as if you turned a geode
inside out like a sock, to hide your grey basalt purpose
inside a bed of violet crystals.

At Home with the Dead

The afterlife at 2 a.m. is a closed
system of memories, a flashlight
that flicks away from the grey
contrivance of consciousness

and lights up another room
where you have been all along,
where you are right now,
unaware of this restless

house, listening to *Ruby Tuesday*
with your legs crossed under you
and every possible year in your face.

I do not claim I can see you
reading maps with a magnifying glass,
a fifth of bourbon on the butcher block
table in this kitchen of yours

that is mine now. I do hear the melody
of an alto recorder that suggests your presence,
though I insist I believe none of it

except your impatient nod
to our old debate, that yesterday
is not gone and matters.

Synesthete

My daughter sings in the primary colors
of her name. Paints with the hum of lightning
bugs on a Pennsylvania night. Calls me in blooming
citrus and cinnabar red.

She fixes each calendar page to its visual
continuum and fastens the day to the horizon
for safe keeping, sure as the equation
is azalea pink every single time.

She warns me when a voice on the air
smells rancid, when water sings a bruise
on the skin, when the sum of numbers
does not equal its counterpart

in the garden of the spoken sky.

Arrest Me Red

Maroon is insipid
in this context. Coral
is close but if you insist
on compromise
there are jaspers

and pinstripes of agate
that elevate this gaudy
impulse to the pretense
of class. I am bone tired
of these nods to elegance.

I've got my hair tied up
in a polka dot scarf
and I'm flying up I-10
in a 68 Charger,
its grill pure cherry sin.

A wide lipstick laugh
at a black asphalt joke.

Against Economy

I know my sin is profusion,
an offense against the polished
geometry that dictates elegance
at the expense of plenty,

though even I agree that blackberry
vines are a nuisance, an empty
beach and single orchid are always
beautiful and squalor never is.

But when your engineer's aesthetic
wants only the necessary and elevates
parsimony to some kind of moral
imperative, I will offer you

walls stacked with books,
fifty years of top 100s,
the spice rack, the studio,
the wood-box and pantry,
guests in the spare room.

Mrs. Nation, Uninvited, Haunts "The Irma"

With a hatchet and a head of pious sabotage
she settles for the rural life and a bar stool
between the skirts of conviviality and the other dead
shot ghosts at The Irma Hotel in Cody, Wyoming.

Never one to appeal to reason, or trust
earnest oversight to a pair of sensible shoes,
she calls the complacent departed to account
and welcomes us all to the dry side of town.

Most of us just blow right past the intrusion
and the newspaperman behind her. We are wise
to the familiar dodge of a man in love
with the fabrication of his wife,

whose perceived goodness eclipses
her flat-eyed certainty and ignites the air
over Buffalo Bill's joint like a curl
of fire inside a rising blue balloon.

Right Behind You

In my nightmare
you could walk again
but before I could
catch up
you were a kite
sailing over Paraguay.

I called in your bird
language
but you were a boy
dancing
with a woman
in the wide-brimmed
hat of her tribe.

I waited
next to a window
that was you
but it was covered
with frost and frozen
shut.

I swear I chased
down every alley
after you, now a black horse
lost in the oil fields of Kuwait
skidding on the grease-slicked
vein of passage.

I woke before
I could coax you
away from the well fires,
the horizon alight
with everything
I hope.

Haboob

This morning I invited the wind into my kitchen
and was accepted after curiosity overruled
the etiquette of dust. I tell you, whole ghost

cultures bolted in defiance of a simple prism hanging
above the sink, which threatened to give offense
by splitting the sun into prophecy, by means of welcome.

From my window I watched the daylight believing
I would recognize the wandering hazard when it cast its cape
around our genial cabal. It is a riot out there, a roil of silica

surging across my forbearance in challenge to the sun,
to the crystal facets that color my walls with the sparkle
of amity, then dissipate before the obligation.

Wait Till the Scorpions Come Out
— for N

You hate the desert and I don't,
it's as simple as that. I point out the red
fruit on a cluster of Christmas cholla,
you show me the pack rat midden
in between. We are both right

but since it is February
and temperate as any June day
on Cape Cod, the point goes to me.
The match will go to you soon enough
in the season I choose to forget

as surely as the serpentine
disaster you saved me from tripping
over last spring and that sting
of recognition from underneath the birdbath
we were foolish enough to move.

1962 Valiant Station Wagon

Aunt Lidie, you handled that thing
like Mr. Magoo and believe me when I say
that the patron saint of close calls was peeking
though her fingers when you made your famous
U-turn on the Falls Bridge at rush hour.

Who could bother with signals and brakes
when, from the rear view, maples lit
by fireflies arched over the East River Drive.
There were Morgan horses from Valley Green
keeping pace along a split rail fence

with the cartoon of your sensible car,
tank half full of City Service regular,
cruising in its cushion of good fortune,
decency and the pure dumb luck of a protected
pilot whale. Grey with fins, red inside.

For Stella on The Day of the Dead

There was no funeral, but we hung bronze
Soleri bells in the palo verde tree that shades
your spot. I thought you might prefer that crazy

sculpture of a bird you bought made of hatchets
and springs, but it sits too heavy on its garden
refuge and we leave fixed to its future.

Instead, we put up a hummingbird feeder
that drips liquid sugar, an offering sweet
as baklava to your final desert home.

We placed a rock shot blue with lapis lazuli
and a sphere of green blown glass. I helped dig
the hole and thought of a poem but never

wrote it down. We offered no prayer
to the afternoon and we did not carve your name.
But each time I make Greek coffee in your copper pot,

I turn over the empty cup as you would have
and read a moment of you in the grounds,
like a psalm.

Stolen From My Father's Room

The family photos pinned to a board by his bed
are gone again. We choose to believe another patient
wandered in and thought she knew the shirtwaist hostess
who was our mother and his wife. She might have recognized
the kid with the crew cut, the quizzical poodle, the child
in the waves.

She may have even smiled at the schmaltz, knowing
a yum yum tree should be aluminum and if that is Uncle
Samuel's son, he could use a haircut. The girl in the miniskirt
might be her own daughter exposed in over-saturated shades
of the Sixties.

We like the fiction of her stuffing those pictures
into her robe as if reclaiming her life. We imagine
it was she, not you, who took them, along with greeting
cards and the blankets I made. Not from anything like
ordinary spite, but from the joy of finding us, her people,
in this place.

Sestina for Zayda and the Dogs

Recently I've noticed that every poem dogs
memory to reveal the parody of a circle
not unlike the trendy mandalas I draw in colored
pencil. Yet I believe that somewhere inside
the circuitry of the stanza, we chase a ghost
that restores the recent past to shades of purple.

Your presence today turned the desert purple.
A shade wide enough for all the house dogs
to rest underneath, unaware of any genial ghost.
These specious hauntings interrupt the circle
that brings me from belief to a place inside
experience, concrete and colored

pink. Each time I laugh and look for a colorful
word in your idiom, I find purple
instead, superstitious and spreading out inside
the spirals of a loss so desolate our dogs
find the corners of closets before they circle
into sleep. I don't believe in anyone's ghost

either, except in verse which is ghost
logic, stories told in relief and colored
by doubt. I will walk straight into that lie only to circle
back to the evening's arroyo, wet and purple
with monsoon rain. It's a wonder the dogs
will do anything but stay inside

ripping a grief I can't see and turning it inside
out. They know the rains come with your ghost
and see shapes lost on everyone but dogs.
They can still hear the discord that colored
your last days and turned mine purple
with regret. They know the edge of the circle

I almost never see, howl at the half circle
of the waxing moon like an inside
joke at the expense of reason. I will seek out purple
now, gather it like lilacs to an antique vase your ghost
would love, leave a path marked in colored
stones for both of us to follow, and scent trails for the dogs.

Our dogs will always circle before lying outside in colored
light, while inside your ghost laughs and resolves to purple.

When the Test to Predict Alzheimer's Is Available

I will be away from my desk
on a road trip to the Wind River Range. I will be drinking
coffee from a cardboard McDonald's cup. Or I will be home,
hanging Marianne's stained glass in the kitchen window or laundry
on a line. I will be kneading sour dough, writing poems or texting dog
pictures to my daughter. Straightening an oil painting of the three of us
in Manzanita, Oregon. Filling the hummingbird feeder. Reading an electronic
book published in 1813. Feeding my fish. Listening to *Ladies of the Canyon*.
I will be crocheting colors of my great grandmother into another new blanket.
Reminding my mother that she changed her password
and my father that I am his daughter
and my name is Sara.

Acknowledgments

A special thanks to the journals where the following poems first appeared:

Instead of a Common Brawl, *Turtle Island Quarterly*, 2017
Stolen From My Father's Room, *Main Street Rag*, 2015
Most Evenings She Searches for a Home, *Crab Creek Review*, 2013
Viscera, *The Smoking Poet*, 2013
What I Did for the Coyote Hunting My Dog, *Vayavya*, 2013
Prayer Wheel, *Turtle Island Quarterly*, 2013
The Pagoda on Yellowstone Highway, *Owen Wister Review*, 2011
Tech Support from My House in Wyoming, 1999, *Antiphon*, 2013
The Poet Turns Las Vegas Into, *Turtle Island Quarterly*, 2013
Rattlesnake, *Turtle Island Quarterly*, 2013
My Father Refuses a Cane, *Avatar Review*, 2012
Sand Painting, *Antiphon*, 2013
A Case for Ghosts, *RE/VERSE*, 2015
Cannibal, *Red River Review*, 2017
Family Geology, *Poppy Road*, 2014
For Stella on the Day of the Dead, *Kentucky Review*, 2015
Arrest Me Red, *Crab Creek Review*, 2013
Against Economy, *Verse Wisconsin*, 2012
Mrs. Nation, Uninvited, Haunts "The Irma," *Poetry Quarterly*, 2014
1962 Valiant Station Wagon, *Verse Wisconsin*, 2012
Haboob, *Ginosko*, 2014
Wait Till the Scorpions Come Out, *The Toucan Magazine*, 2014
Synesthete, *Turtle Island Quarterly*, 2016
When the Test To Predict Alzheimer's Is Available, *Kentucky Review*, 2014

The cover photo "Rain on Glass 1" by William K. Kates first appeared in *Houseboat*, 2012

About the Author

Sara Clancy is a Philadelphia transplant to the Desert Southwest by way of two lovely detours through Wyoming and Washington State. She was a bookseller and a support technician for graphic design software; she went to college and graduate school far too long ago to mention. She is an associate editor for *Good Works Review*. Sara's poems have appeared, among other places, in *Off the Coast*, *The Linnet's Wings*, *Poppy Road*, *Kentucky Review*, *Crab Creek Review*, *Antiphon*, *Verse Wisconsin*, *Pirene's Fountain*, *Turtle Island Quarterly*, and *Houseboat*, where she was a featured poet. She lives in Arizona with her husband, their two dogs, a cross-eyed cat, and a 24 year old goldfish named Darryl.

www.ingramcontent.com/pod-product-compliance
Lightning Source LLC
Chambersburg PA
CBHW072040060426
42449CB00010BA/2376